Red Devon

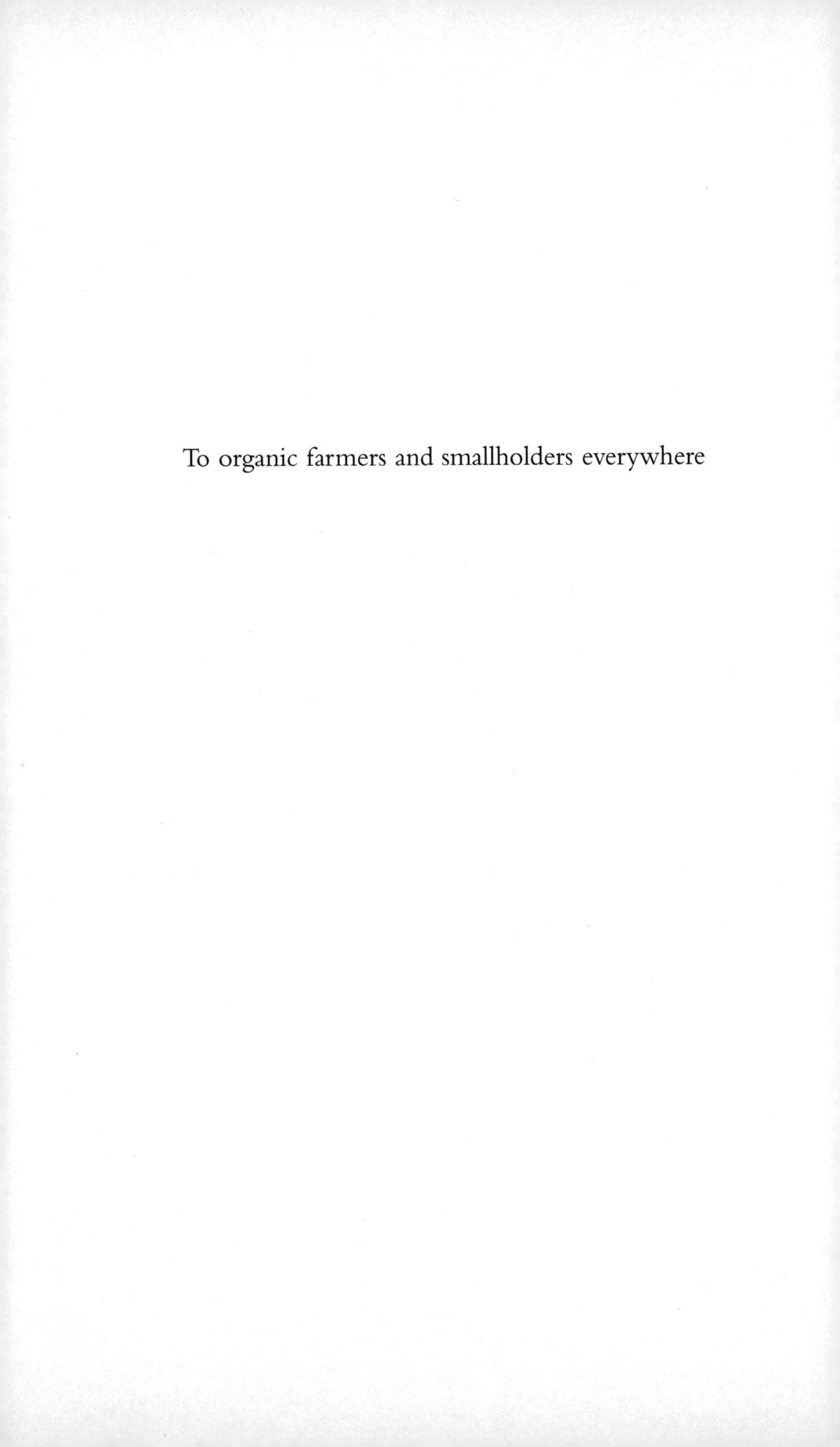

To organic farmers and smallholders everywhere

Hilary Menos
Red Devon

SEREN

Seren is the book imprint of
Poetry Wales Press Ltd.
57 Nolton Street, Bridgend, Wales, CF31 3AE
www.serenbooks.com
Facebook: facebook.com/SerenBooks
Twitter: @SerenBooks

ISBN print: 978-1-78172-054-7
ISBN kindle: 978-1-78172-056-1
ISBN e-book: 978-1-78172-055-4

A CIP record for this title is available from the British Library.

The publisher acknowledges the financial assistance of the Welsh Books Council.

Cover photograph: Shastajak

Printed in Bembo by Berforts Group, Stevenage.

Author's Website: http://www.hilarymenos.co.uk/

Contents

The Ballad of Grunt Garvey and Jo Tucker

Shambles

UK 364195

The Ballad of Grunt Garvey and Jo Tucker

The secret of a good ley is a firm bottom
– Devon farming proverb

Being Grunt Garvey

Winsome is sixteen today. She sprawls
like a crumpled ballerina straddling the drainage gully
while her sisters mill around and munch hay.

Grunt brooms slurry off the concrete floor.
There's more than one way to skin a cow
but, this being Grunt Garvey, he will do it the one way

and sling her from the spike with webbing strops
like the special delivery under a stork's beak
or Darcey Bussell performing a grand jeté.

It could all go wrong. I see her paddling the air,
the noose – which it is – too high, too low, or both
and, this being Grunt Garvey, things don't go to plan –

she proves to be quite the Houdini, although
it's rather more than two minutes thirty-six seconds
before she hits the straw with a wet thud.

Grunt goes for the JCB with the gap-toothed scoop
to shovel her up like chippings, or so much grain.
Of course it can't go wrong, but this being, etc.

she rolls in like a set of bagpipes with a low moan,
steam from her paunch soft-focussing her face
and more than a little damage to her tail bone.

Midday tomorrow, if she's not on her feet
(*on pointes* if you're chasing the extended metaphor)
the local knackerman will bring his gun

and attempt a short duet
before Winsome struts her stuff for the last time
along the tightrope of his winch and chain

into his tatty van. For those familiar with the charm
of a cow's final *fouetté*,
this is a good time to look away.

* grand jeté – *a ballet term indicating a long horizontal jump*
* on pointes – *dancing on the tips of the toes*
* fouetté – *a quick whipping around of the body from one direction to another*

Knackerman

Rattling down the lane comes John Teague,
eager to please, eager to do his job,
partly because he is four days late
and the ewe dumped by the shed is on the turn.

Don't ask him what he knows,
John Teague, with his aura of flies,
one eye up the chimney, one eye down the pot,
leaving nothing but a damp stain on the road.

He knows the inside of a pig's mind.
To put his gun to the back of a ram's head.
How a cow falls to her knees as if in prayer
in this reverse nativity in a half-dark byre.

Burgoo

"You got livestock, you got dead stock," hollers Grunt.
He slams the tailgate, waves Teague off the farm.
Stan from Stags has come to talk about forms
and how everyone's going to die of BSE.

In the kitchen Stan's telling Dad about New Variant CJD.
Grunt makes mugs of instant on the Rayburn.
Mum says she knows a man with a sponge for a brain.
Dad says he knows a mad cow

but they must be proper mental in Kentucky,
eating road-kill varmints in a stew.
"A few ears short of a bushel," says Stan,
"and five of them dead too."

What sort of varmints, Grunt wants to know.
"Used to be squirrel or possum," says Stan,
"but these days it's beef or lamb."
New Variant burgoo.

"Eggs and brains," says Mum, "the butcher's treat,
we had that every week when we were young."
"No wonder your brains are scrambled," says Grunt,
and throws his slops down the sink.

That night they sit out, skimming stones on the slurry.
Teague says, "Remember the road-kill kid,
spit-roast rats, hedgehogs wrapped in mud,
what happened to him?"

"We had a fight in woodwork once," says Grunt,
"he tried to cut off my head with a junior hacksaw.
But he got diabetes and moved to Ugborough.
What goes around comes around."

"After all that squirrel stew," says Teague,
"reckon he's not coming round no more."

* burgoo - *traditional North American stew made with whatever meat is available*
* BSE - *Bovine spongiform encephalopathy, a fatal neurodegenerative disease in cattle*
* CJD - *Creutzfeldt–Jakob disease, a fatal degenerative neurological disorder in humans*
* New Variant CJD - *When BSE infects humans, the resulting disease is (new) variant CJD*

Grunt's Bane

One foot in the furrow, one on the grassed ridge,
he strolls lopsided, sniffs at pineapple mayweed,
listens as stonechats crack pebbles in the hedge,
counts on his fingers how thistles annex his land.

Spear thistles rattle their sabres in open scrub.
Dwarf thistles lurk in the couch, planning a raid.
Spotted thistles infest his set aside, their sly lobes
and pale flowers colonising his waysides.

Tall bull thistle, creeping thistle, tuberous and woolly,
nodding in the pastures, inching across his red loam,
crowding the shaled edge of the old quarry,
sharper than hoof picks, tougher than baler twine.

Blessed and bitter, cursed and holy, milk and melancholy,
lady's thistle, slender thistle, each and every one Grunt's bane.

Wheelbarrow Farm

When hell freezes over, he swears by three things.
Lard on the lips. Two pairs of socks. His wheelbarrow,
good on the steep when even the Ford won't grip.

This morning he opens the door to a clean sweep
right up to the dairy's cracked slate step, frost
spangling the tank and, briefly, he's ten years old

but now it's taking the piss. Grunt glares at the snow
and it glares back. He kicks the water trough,
heels a hole through the ice. First floods, now this,

the daily round, in arctic sludge. Milk substitute
for the calves, a brick of pellets for the fowls.
He rolls out a silage bale in the cubicle house

and forks it to the cows, sets a can at the yard tap
drumming up chilly water for the dogs,
for the lambs in the barn, the fifty hogs on the hill.

A neighbour phones on the scrounge for a box
and a tow out of the ditch where he spent the night.
Grunt goes off to do what he does best –

apply excess force with a tool. He's back at noon
to fix a burst pipe, by which time two sheep
haven't moved for an hour, are past fixing.

Snow starts to fall as he toils up the slope,
hauls one sheep into the wheelbarrow,
picks his way down, then moils up again.

Mates Rates

Grunt's not any sort of man.
But if he was, he'd be the sort
– if you were digging a hole –
not to sit back and watch the show

but to step up to the mark,
place his hand gently on your arm,
take your spade and offer you
the key to his digger. Mates Rates.

The Blue Hour

The fence between Pullheads and Hatchet came down,
each post rottener than the last, and both flocks together –
ewes, lambs, wethers – and there on the high ground

centre stage, the two rams squaring up to each other
each without armour or lance, just a curled helm
and the action between them unfolding.

Grunt's seen year-olds jockeying in a pen – the short run,
the butt and buck and high kick, the gradual retreat
that heralds a new order in the fold – and he's seen

the old ram in the orchard earnestly thumping the trees
until small green apples pelt the barreners beneath,
and all from a standing start. So he's drinking his tea

and starting to think about getting the dogs
when a noise he associates most with a scaffold bar,
or a length of four by two, fractures the scene.

They stagger apart, each ram looking crossly around
for applause, perhaps, or a swift way out
or a "Cut!" from the director. But there is none.

So they back up and do it again, shoulder to shoulder,
lurching into each other like Friday night drunks,
or huddled like boxers against the crowd's urging

and each one's nervous twitch sends the other
further up the field and a little further
until each backs up almost out of the frame

and they do it again, only better, and this time both
fall, a double whammy in long shot slow motion,
and the lights all dim, and the evening rolls on in.

* barreners – *barren ewes*
* wethers – *castrated male sheep*

Colin

Up at four to milk and the Dartmouth lights
glow yellow down the valley. Hay for the calves,
barley for the pigs and the yard to scrape.
Clouds of mist form with each breath.

He picks out lambs for market. Backs up the box
and shoves them in by hand. For once they're quiet.
Then out with the old plough bobbing behind.
Five shining blades. The tractor rears and strains.

There's winter wheat to walk, lime to spread,
the barn to clear before the auction date.
The quad bike's got no brakes. The lad's off sick
so that's another weekend spoken for.

Headlights blazing, mind a blank, he ploughs
long after dark. Post on the doormat, untouched.

Rammed

Grunt barrows each ram to its own pen in the shed
near Peg, the in-lamb ewe with the broken leg,
though he needn't have bothered: one lies in the straw

shaking, not even as good as dead meat,
the other scrabbles the air with its front feet,
eyes bled black, unable to stand or walk.

By midnight the shaking stops. What little breath
comes short and slow. Grunt's seen enough
to know where this one's heading, and when it's due.

The other watches with a mixture of fear and scorn,
pressed against the hurdles, its curved horns
heavy on its neck, its slack back end askew.

Grunt fetches a bottle of Life Aid from the meds box,
drops by the all-night vet for some steroid shots,
brings water and an armful of horse hay,

then hauls the live one up till it half stands, half leans,
drags itself after him, bluffing and harrying his knees
even as its back legs slide under and away.

Two days later Peg lambs. Grunt cuts her cast
and eases open the wadding and crumbled plaster.
Watching her test the bone as her two lambs feed,

their tails a-shimmy, each one nuzzling a teat,
Grunt reckons the ram's had time. He speed dials Teague
as he's shepherding Peg and her lambs back into the field

and gets home from ploughing that night to find
three empty pens, an hour off his daily round,
and only a field full of healthy sheep to mind.

The Great Hog Oiler Round Up

Colin bought it at a farm sale in Iowa.
A nineteen-fifteen Lisle Swine-Ezer Hog Oiler.

"The Pig Farmer's Best Defense Against Mange and Lice,"
said Colin. A divorce present for his ex-wife.

Now it squats in Grunt's garden like a fire hydrant
or stocky pillar box, glistening with tractor paint.

Grunt leafs through the vintage catalogue, keen to buy
their blunt promise – Hog Joy, Health Hog, Rub Hog Or Die,

coveting one shaped like an outsize billiard ball
snug in its sump, nineteen-twelve, patent applied for.

So many scrapped, or rusting in ditches and barns,
the weight – and the history – of their cast iron forms

worth less than a powder puff dusting of lindane
(moderately hazardous). "Like the wife," says Colin.

The Harrowing

Armed with bolt cutters, gauntlets and hand-held winch,
he starts third time lucky, cursing the dodgy earth,
backs up to join the harrow to the three point linkage.

It looks like a folding bedstead, the weave of the chain
like Qs with tails worn bright. Its counterweight
sends his front wheels bouncing all over the lane.

He starts at the top of the hill, raking the bents
for thistles and stroil grass and thatch. He likes this part.
He circles the field once more, then starts his descent.

At the bottom, one thick wheel broadsides the sedge
and the back of the harrow swings out and snags
on something anchored deep in the blackthorn hedge.

It feels as if hands are sucking him into the redshank,
an ancestor ploughed up and out of his cold barrow,
or offended by the grubbing up of an ancient bank.

Grunt slams the diff lock on with a curse and a prayer
and the tractor lurches and tips. Mud spatters his face
as the wheels churn, and churn, until he pulls away

dragging a tangle of wire and posts strung together
– the buried results of years of winter fencing –
a barbed necklace fit for some monstrous mother.

He parks in the yard back down at the farm in the valley
where bees nose orchids and white campion
and the cadences of the church bells barely carry,

opens the kitchen door, still sweating from his trial,
a dark hulk against the light, a mud-reamed troglodyte,
and sits down with a 'Value' pizza in front of Countryfile.

Badger Season

Grunt has Dad's old Webley & Scott twelve bore
with the dinged end and the open scroll chasing on the stock,
the right barrel choked by three quarters,
the left choked by a half, for close work.

Teague has his usual .22 for the fox
and his .243 because you never know when...
(he mutters something inaudible about Brock)
and – for fun with rabbits – he's brought his four ten.

Both fancy trying their luck down at Rolster Bridge
but Colin's trying to impress some bird he met online
by taking her lad lamping that side of the ridge
so they sit for a while in the car watching the moon

and comparing guns. Teague likes a ballistic head
which shatters on impact, leaving no trace. Grunt says
last year testing left thirty-five thousand cattle dead
so frankly anything goes; vaccination, poison, gas.

Far off down the valley they hear a vixen howl
calling her mate. After an hour they go back to the farm.
The sheep are grey ghosts in the kale,
their eyes bright dots reflecting the Clulite's beam.

Grunt sends in the kelpie. She looks like a fox.
He's saying how easy it is – the glint through your sight
could be the eye of a fox, or a torch face,
or a button. Even a mobile phone reflects light,

and these days kids are always – when a shot
cracks round the hills like a whip cracked right.
Teague raises his gun towards Rolster Bridge in salute
to what they both reckon is one less black-and-white.

They are in the field that Grunt has just cut for grass
when something whirls overhead, low and close by,
rotor blades slicing segments out of the stars
and a searchlight roving the hillside like one bright eye

that has both men and beasts running for cover.
After that there's nothing moving, so they go home.
Grunt is paunching rabbits in the yard when it goes back over
and he glances up as it passes, its low drone

sending the dog whimpering under the Fendt,
making his own teeth rattle and his stomach vibrate.
The trademark red and blue of the air ambulance
soaks the hills all around in crimson light.

He puts the meat in the fridge and turns on the PC
for a game of his favourite shoot-em-up, 'Badger Season.'
As he blasts the black-and-whites red, the events of the evening
fall into place like cartridges into a gun,

the soft click into the breech, the gentle squeeze,
and a bad call which blows everything to kingdom come.

* lamping – *hunting rabbits or other nocturnal animals using off-road cars and high powered lights*
* to paunch a rabbit – *to remove the innards*

Full Load

The rumour runs round the parish like a case of lice:
the Garveys have gone down with TB.
Even Teague admits he doesn't know for sure
but at seven this morning Jo Tucker, thirty-three,
the best haulier for miles and not just on price

points her truck towards the Garvey's place.
The verge runs red with rain and the Devon mud.
She flips the wipers on to double speed,
turns the radio on and, as the road starts to flood,
drops down a gear and slows to walking pace.

Been a while since Jo has driven down this way.
A line of young alders has sprung up along the brook
and a new gateway gapes in an old hedge
fresh laid with a chainsaw and baler twine for crooks.
Garvey's farmhouse squats in a veil of grey.

Grunt, in waterproofs, heaven diluting his tea,
stands by the slate porch. Jo Tucker steels
herself for the sight of Grunt's face. Just one look
and she doesn't need to ask, can already feel
the awful weight of a full load to Hatherleigh.

She backs up to the shed and drops the ramp,
slots the side gates in as Grunt opens the doors
and they watch the cows come out and sniff the air.
They smell of good grass and good straw,
the smoky molasses stink of Grunt's silage clamp.

Grunt goes to push them on in but Jo says to wait,
there's plenty of room in the truck. She walks past
working their flight zone, and the cows move on
slipping a bit on the wet ramp. At last
they are all in and she slams the partition gate.

"One more to come," says Grunt, his face a blank
and out of the shed looms his Red Devon bull.
The truck rocks as he walks in, his head low,
the knock and echo of his hooves terrible,
sweat on his nose and shoulders and muscled flank.

Jo starts the truck, fighting something like horror,
and pulls away, wheels briefly adrift in the mire
only then daring to glance back at Grunt in the lane
staring at her, at the truck, hands loose at his sides,
getting smaller and smaller in her rear-view mirror.

Kingdom Come

At market the talk is all about Colin and his
six-month sentence suspended for two years

and the boy
and the other boys

Tom who took the tractor for a swim
Dick who fell in the sheep dip
Harry rolled flat by round bale hay

the wives who drown in grain silos
flailing in bullion like calves in a slurry pit

brothers winched away by an unguarded drive shaft
or last seen dancing on overhead power lines.

"Closer to thee, my Lord," says Teague.
"Skip, trip or fall," says Grunt.

Trapped by stacked material
Uncontrolled exposure to poultry dust
Manslaughter by gross negligence

"Meant the world to him, that boy," says Teague.
They observe a minute's silence.
"And to top it all, he's disqualified from holding a shotgun licence."

Once Upon a Time in the West

As Jo hands an entry form to the market men
she clocks Grunt unloading fat lambs in the pennage.

Waiting to wash out, she's behind him in the queue,
parks alongside his Bateson, plotting a duel.

Two quid for the lad. She grabs the high pressure hose
and gets a squirt in quick while Grunt is still dozy.

He's right back at her, gets her full blast in the chest
then it's back and forth like a Spaghetti Western

until Grunt surrenders, hands reaching for the sky,
Jo's barrel cocked at his groin and ready to fire.

The effect of Grunt's smile wasn't part of Jo's plan
– Sedgemoor livestock market is no place for romance –

but when Grunt offers lunch "for the sharpest shooter"
Jo flushes bright red and finds herself strangely mute.

A Load of Old Bull

One deliberate hoof tests the ramp. Head low,
the bull shoulders out of the slant shadow,

sashays into the pen with a swagger,
muscled like a bovine Schwarzenegger,

and leans on the gate, enjoying the strain.
"Seven hundred quid," says Grunt. "A bargain.

And if he brings me any sort of fight
he'll be off quicker than a bride's nightie."

In the late sun, Grunt and the bull glow red.
Midges dance a garland around their heads.

Driving home, Jo broods on the loading bay,
four blokes with sticks, the seller's cagey eye

and wonders what postscripts have been added
to the given pattern of this old bull's blood.

New Blood

Grunt says he got him for a good price.
Jo says, "Buy cheap, buy twice."
Grunt says, "Better buy than borrow."
Jo says, "Buy in haste, in leisure sorrow."

Grunt says, "Pedigree blood for pedigree seed."
Jo says, "Better a good bull than a bull of a good breed"
and "Many a good cow hath an ill calf."
Grunt says, "Have you seen his EBV percentiles graph?"

Grunt says he took a first at the County Show.
"Handsome is as handsome does," says Jo.
Grunt says the vendor is switching to A.I.
Jo says, "Half the truth is often a lie."

Grunt says he covered fifty cows last year.
Jo says, "Naught so brisk as bottled beer."
and "They that promise quick, perform slow.
Speak as I find," says Jo.

Shoot Supper

There have been two, maybe three, other men for Jo.
She'd say "mind your own" if you asked her who.
There have been two, maybe three, other women for Grunt
but not lately. He confronts the mirror, splashes on Brut,
digs out his one good suit and is good to go.

Jo rakes through her wardrobe, twice, but nothing appeals.
Weeks, she's been waiting for this – like an old fool –
the one day of the year Grunt's off duty in a public place.
She looks in the mirror, checks her face, her arse.
"A Devon heifer," she mutters. "Beef to the heels."

It's boy-girl-boy at the supper. John Teague
sits up straight all night admiring Jo's cleavage
until Colin invites him outside to see his new pick-up.
Jo empties her glass for courage, and another for luck
and the evening starts to come unstuck. She has vague

impressions of Grunt laughing, Grunt filling her glass,
his arm warm on the back of her chair, his eyes amused,
his smile lopsided like a tick, a sum well done,
and she decides to take the chance before it's gone,
leans forward to kiss him (just do it!) bold as brass.

Jo lets herself in back home, quietly, late.
Sees herself in the mirror in a different light.
She's clutching a napkin covered with Grunt's rough scrawl.
A map to a meeting place, a car park on the moor.
Not quite the romance she'd been hoping for. But a date.

Tercio de Muerte

Blokes in this business would write Grunt as Theseus.
Godlike (him being a god) he grapples the bull,
lugs it to London to parade along Pall Mall
then coolly butchers it in the name of Reason.

Or Grunt as Toreador, humble but worthy
practitioner of fine art playing to the stands,
his suit of lights coruscating against beige sands,
dealing hard truths in the Tercio de Muerte.

Or Grunt as bull-runner, giving the beast the slip,
vaulting or somersaulting honed handlebar horns,
depicted in a mosaic, a fresco or as a carved figurine
in a rite of passage, an initiation ritual, or act of worship.

So much for history, then. Teague found him huddled
at the foot of the shed wall, flail chest, not a moan,
crumpled in all the wrong places. Grunt as dead man.
But how it was, after the first broadside hustle,

when things started to get... how to put it... ugly,
when that great head, that alien will of iron
kept on coming for Grunt, what flashed before his eyes,
what he was thinking, no-one knows. Not even me.

The Ballad of Grunt Garvey and Jo Tucker

Oh for a story as simple as boy meets girl
with a love that lasts and a future little Jo
who walks plastic cows up the ramp of her toy truck
while little Grunt waves a stick to make them go.

At eight Jo parks, unfolds and folds the map,
listens to the metal tick as the big truck cools.
Low sun flames the gorse. A buzzard mews.
How does she feel? How do you think she feels?

I wanted so much more for Jo than this
slow lengthening of shadows, this swift descent
winding her way back home through chilly lanes
trying to guess what was or wasn't meant.

And still to come: the horror of Grunt's yard.
Jo standing unacknowledged in the crowd.

Shambles

Poets and pigs are appreciated only after their death
– Italian proverb

Agnus Scythicus

Also known as the Vegetable Lamb of Tartary, this legendary animal/plant hybrid was believed to grow sheep as a fruit. In medieval times it was used to explain the existence of cotton.

Here in God's Own Country, our harvests are legend.
From John Mandeville to Gulliver, travelers flock
to rhapsodise the fruits of our sun-kissed ground.

The jewel in our crown is the Vegetable Lamb
which springs skyward on a single artichoke stalk,
pendulous limbs hanging slack from a fleece-blurred bloom.

Each fruit is wrapped in a boll of whisked wool
to protect it from wolves. When the monsoon smiles
water pours from the pods like silk from a spool.

The umbilicus bends to allow the lamb to graze
as far as the cord goes, on nard and camomile.
It circles daintily on hooves of parted hair.

People in God's Own Country borrow and sow, sow
and borrow, attended by thrip and moth and worm
all keen to help light traps and trenches overflow

while our children fall like fruit from the neem trees,
gasping for breath. Bees refuse to sting or swarm,
and the last cows rock-and-roll and kick up their heels.

Under the banyan a girl licks her lips and stares
slow as molasses in spring. Beside her, a boy,
whose strange, bifurcated hands reach for the stars.

Witches' Broom

Witches' Broom Disease ravaged cocoa plantations in South America in the 1980s.

It came on the wind, on the sole of somebody's shoe,
on the blade of a machete. And before you could say "stout Cortez"
spores were forming alliances under the canopy.

It spread like a secret. Our trees grew ears.
We watched their biochemistry unravel, limb by limb,
the ineluctable shift of gold from host to pathogen.

Now every pod is empty. What can we do?
Fill our gourds with annatto, so our mouths are a red stain?
Burn the fat to the devil? The old Gods don't listen, don't hear,

caught between a rock and a prickly pear.
Ours is bitter water, washed down with bitter certainties,
and everything swept away by these new brooms.

Shambles

This is the cow that peered down the black hole of the captive bolt
shrugged its clod against the head-gate
and said, like Gary Gilmour facing a five-man firing squad in
Utah State,
"Let's do it!"

This is the sheep that held out a hoof
as the tongs ear-muffed her temples
and said, like John Amery greeting the hangman in Wandsworth
Gallows,
"Oh Mr Pierrepoint, I've always wanted to meet you
but not, of course, under these circumstances."

This is the goat that, incompletely stunned,
offered his throat to the knife
and said, like Walter Raleigh mentally thumbing the axe,
"So the heart be right, it is no matter which way the head lieth."

This is the chicken that, shackled by one foot to the rack,
reached the electric bath for a partial KO
and said, like Tony Mancini receiving the hood at Pentonville
Prison,
"Cheerio."

And this is the pig that, trotting through the race to the gas cubicle,
put down his regulation-issue Bible
and said, like Sean Patrick Flanagan readying his arm
in a small white room in Nevada,
"I love you."

Pigweed

Remember the pigweed in twenty-twelve
decimating our corn. Our bean crop, halved.

Farming forums debated lost wheat yields
while combines ground to a halt in the fields.

Shoots elbowed up through gravel and concrete.
Cotton was throttled. Ploughs broke, harrows bent.

Six foot trespassers thick as a man's thigh
cocked a snook at all of our pesticides.

The only advice was "sharpen your hoes."
We put chopping crews in to work the rows.

So much for science and its magic wand.
Ever cleared a million acres by hand?

Where we were headed was anyone's guess
once the weeds had worked out how to resist.

★

The white coats brainstormed a cluster of tricks –
overlapping residuals, tank mix,

burn-down, pre- and post-emergence programs –
all old tactics in a frightening new game.

Some tried to turn back to the good old ways –
cover crops, green mulches, long-term grass leys,

seven year rotations rebuilding soil,
pre-PKN, pre-chemicals, pre-oil –

but as marestail, waterhemp and rye grass
ganged up for a triple-headed advance

we privately knew we had lost the race,
caught here between a rock and a hard place.

Thanks to the pigweed in twenty-thirteen
we harvested famine, famine, famine.

★

We needed a new approach. That's where I
came in, an old ranch hand able to fly

twenty-four/seven, under the radar
no baggage, no pack drill, codename hades,

with a great big tank of something orange
tucked in my old Provider's fuselage.

Don't ask me what I know. All I can say
is you can't get proper coverage today

with your bog-standard tractor mounted rig
and Dad says faint heart never fucked a pig.

What do I see when coming in to land?
Black rags spiraling upwards on the wind

far in the distance, past any spray arm.
Rooks winding water. Heavy rain to come.

Pietà

In Paraguay toxic pesticides on GM soy affects the health of people living nearby. Women living within 1km of sprayed fields are twice as likely to have a child with deformities.

There is nothing littoral
    here. A green tide
covers the yard, the garden, the bosque,
washes against the casa wall,
    right up to the built edge.
Open the back door and you are besieged.
    Spray colonises the air.

They acted like gods, and we
    beckoned them down.
Like members of the old cargo cults
cutting runways through the Chaco,
    each wearing a headset
manufactured from cassava and corn,
    and imitating semaphore.

We kissed the toad. Now we are
    swallowing it.
Asphalt ribbons quarter the fields. What
was once patchwork is now chessboard
    and on such a scale that
renders most of us speechless. In this place,
    there is a kind of plenty,

in the blue of the babies,
    their lust to land,
the arrangements of small limbs, the sheer
variety of arrangements,
    things that go right up to
and beyond the edge, and on a scale that
    renders most of us speechless.

Kissing Cousins

When your heart is broken I will give you my heart.
Got yourself a living, walking source of spare parts.

Your table bears my meat, your body my tanned hide.
My blood thickens your pudding, my lard slicks your bread.

I am friend and foe and flesh, sacred and profane,
my head on a pole, my spleen as a weather vane.

You are my maker, from conception to sticking,
crooning a lullaby or skewered on a spit,

and I'm yours, from snout to tail, from belly to loin,
yielding my brawn for your brawn, my brain for your brain.

I am suckled and relished, forbidden and cursed,
close a cousin as you like and never been kissed.

Brush-makers, saddlers, cobblers all tap-tap away
while this little piggy goes "Wee-wee-wee-wee-wee."

Red Tide

A 'red tide' occurs when algae grow so fast the water appears red.
Algal blooms can result in fish kill.

Something was going on. I lay awake in bed
dreaming of biblical plagues – a river of blood

bled from efflorescences of force-fed algae –
woke fixed on the finer points of allegory

and saw, dead in the water, more than a million
blunt-lipped silverlings, a sprawled apron of chain mail.

We shoveled bucket loads, barrow loads, trawled and tipped
them, hissing, on tarps draped over a row of skips,

toenail clippings from a horde of iron giants.
When the mess was clear, we got down to the science,

wrestled with agricultural run-off and wind,
but all the white coats could make of it in the end

was a slap-up supper for five thousand seals.
One miracle gone belly up with a bad smell.

Dead Zone

Dead zones are hypoxic (low-oxygen) areas in oceans and lakes often caused by nutrient pollution from agricultural run-off.

So we chucked a couple of pigs over the side,
cameras recording the rate at which they decayed.

On day one we got just what we were expecting.
The porkers lay on the ocean floor, unblinking.

On day two we got crabs, day three shrimp and plumed worm.
Then a dozen sea stars inched in for the long game.

Last to arrive were squat lobsters, flexing fanned tails,
claws working the pigs over like pneumatic drills.

No sharks, no orcas, just humble bottom feeders
restoring proper chaos to this strange order.

Come summer, the sea water warmed, the plankton bloomed
and even the crabs shuffled off into the gloom.

One starfish remains, dark matter in the thick brine,
too used to thin air, fondly clasping a jaw bone.

Long Pig

We eat the flesh only in wartime, when enraged,
and in a few legal instances. Theft. Treason.

Adultery. When the elders deem fit, revenge.
When a captured prisoner cannot pay ransom

in coin or woman or pig. And we find nothing
animates missionaries like being eaten.

When we introduce you to the village elders,
you men, with your degrees from Oxford and Eton,

must squat at the far end of the hut from our king
due to your woeful lack of pigs. Still, be at ease.

But when our women gather salt, and limes, and rice,
hanging coconuts like sucked skulls from the palm trees,

it might be prudent to invoke the Lord's Prayer twice,
or whatever prayer, to whatever God you please.

Operation Blessing

In 1978 the pigs of Haiti were diagnosed with Asian Swine Flu and were eradicated. The repopulation program had mixed results.

Good God, who has ears to hear, we are being blessed
again as for centuries we have been so blessed,

so often relieved of the burdens of freedom,
and now of our pigs, who were rude, necessary

and blessed. They were our banks, our goods, our ancestors,
with snouts like ploughs and dung rich and robust

like the coffee we grew before we became blessed.
Now we are further blessed with these useless Iowan

beasts, these *princes à quatre pieds* whose empty breasts
and soft stomachs shrivel in our yards, whose high heels

balk at our tough scrub, who eat only wheat-based
vitamin-supplemented better-than-we-eat food,

whose thin skin blisters and burns in the Creole sun.
Of all our blessings, good God, this has been the best.

Pig Out

March 2011: China's largest meat processor apologises when the illegal additive clenbuterol – used by bodybuilders and supermodels – is found in its pork products.

It's not like I was a gear head. Some of the swine
have pincushion glutes, lose bowel control at times.

Yeah you bet I had hypertension, the pressure
to be bigger, pinker, leaner – you get nowhere

as a natural these days and you know what they say –
the mountains are high, the emperor far away.

I was starting a cycle of clen, two weeks on,
two off, with taurine supplements and ketofen

when the order came. The driver pissed for us all.
We're half way to Henan when the inspector calls,

sees us sweating like rapists. Runs tests. I end up
fatter than ever, metabolism scuppered,

in hock to these unpredictable fits and starts,
the lub-dub lub-pause-dub of my overblown heart.

UK 364195

Q: How do you know when a farmer has gone organic?
A: Lights on the sprayer tractor

Q: Twenty sheep in the field. One gets out. How many are left?
A: None

Bob's Dogs

There was the one dog, neither use nor ornament.
Each morning he lurked by the tanker's dribbling spout
licking his chops. Spawned every cur in the district.
Bit the postman, once, and got away with it.

There was the other dog, two-bit brother to the first,
eyes like spilt milk. Danced on the slurry pit's crust
one time too many, said Bob, and no good since.
Bit the builder's foreman twice, and got away with it.

There was the third dog, each month went walkabout
under a chicken moon, fetching and shedding stars.
Deaf to everyone but Bob's dad, now four years
bed-bound. What shall I say? Bit nobody, yet.

And lastly there was the bitch. Bit the child.
The four shots blew through the lanes and echoed loud
in the neighbour's eyes. Only Bob shook my hand,
hitching his trousers up with a "Welcome, my friend."

Stock Take

At first he can't understand how we have another ten
cows this year when we haven't bought any in.

Did he concentrate only in maths
and further maths

staring out of the classroom window during biology
past the perverse arithmetic of one-plus-one-makes-three,

analysing birds, auditing bees,
appraising the net asset value of flowers and grass and trees,

writing them down, writing them off?
And I feel I'm not being euphemistic enough

when I explain the absence of four or five lambs
by saying we ate them.

But when I tell him our kelpie sheepdog followed my car
half way to South Brent at thirty miles an hour

and got picked up by the dog warden in Diptford
and had to be sprung from the pound for forty quid

he insists on entering it as consultancy/legal fees.
"That dog's too good for petty cash," he says.

The Organic Farming Calendar

January

Iconic robin
nib deep in a fat-ball
sings a schmaltzy song.

February

Late nights in the barn
put me off my Sunday roast –
early season lamb.

March

Equinoctal sun
transubstantiates slurry –
black crust to wine gold.

April

The cruelest month.
Our neighbours' NPK grass
is always greener.

May

A froth of blossom
on a black hedgerow.
Good things come to those who wait.

June

Pale and shivering,
ewes leave their golden fleeces
warm on the shed floor.

July

Gloucestershire Old Spots
basking in the midday sun
wallow in Piz Buin.

August

In every meadow
we make hay while the sun shines
literally speaking.

September

Harvest festival.
The altar overflows with
tinned vegetable soup.

October

Bottling cider.
Recipe for disaster:
two spoons of sugar.

November

Farmer in the wind
ploughing a lonely furrow
to Radio One.

December

Seven in a line
goose goose goose goose goose goose goose
the barn floor a quilt.

Woodcock Hay

Cuckoo oats and woodcock hay
makes a farmer run away
– old Cornish proverb

Sugars peak at midsummer then fall as the nights draw in
and for the third year in a row we're entering August
with the hay barn empty but for some bought-in straw
and your motorbike wedged in a corner stall.

We lose patience and cut on a rumour. Rain threatens all day,
the Met Office map sprouting clouds and the odd blue drop
until out of the grey comes summer and the meadows buzz
with a mob of machines, all laying up futures in grass.

The Massey steams out of the shed like a red dragon,
the Bamford baler behind it a triumph of '70s calibration,
part Wallace and Grommit, part Heath Robinson,
the pick up all of a pother, the chute dropping sweet oblongs

onto the stubble. This is grace consecrated in metal,
grab arms gathering, hydraulics shunting the hay
to the needles, knotters, cutters, in precise sequence,
their neat fit the only magic we know or need.

Portrait of the Artist as Venus Anadyomene

Let's get one thing straight. I'm not nude.
I'm dressed in overalls, boots, old leather coat and
(if you're still painting a picture of me in your mind)
drench in one hand, pitchfork in the other.

I'm looking straight at you. Less 'come hither' more
'come and have a go if you think you're hard enough.'
I'm a modern woman. Out of respect for the genre
(and because I'm writing this stuff) I have great hair.

From Eve to Madonna, always, the main question
is what to do with my arms. Loose at my sides?
Raised up over my head to foreground my breasts
or modestly cupping my pubes? You decide. I can

do kneeling, reclining, upright at a tilt, or thigh deep
wringing bronze tresses into a painterly sea.
Between you and me, mostly I'll take contraposto
but lose the nymphs; I'm attended by dead sheep.

Meet me half way in this small white space
and I'll show you a good time girl, a real Goddess,
not love in the abstract, soft porn or cheap romance,
or one of your hostile fractured Cubist tarts

but a multi-dimensional farmyard demoiselle
born from this savoury agricultural soup.
I skim the soft foam perking the slurry's crust
borne across the lagoon on a tractor-mounted dirt scoop.

Roses shower the barn roofs as I shudder to a halt.
The year-old heifers in the cubicle house shift and shit.
Maybe you find this erotic, maybe not.
I'm not what you expected? Deal with it.

⋆*Contraposto* – a pose where the weight rests on one leg, freeing the other, which is bent at the knee

Aileen

We'd never known a summer night so bright,
the moon casting a pooled spot around Aileen,
in labour proper after a day of false starts,
foursquare and straining, her breath fraught.

We knew something was wrong when the two hooves
framing the stubby snout had been poised to dive
for hours from the womb's brutal heave upon heave
and this endless standing up and lying down.

As her fight ebbed we tied calving ropes to the hocks
and braced ourselves for the damp slab of shadow,
the lilac gums and tongue,
                                        then the dross, the dreck,
fine veins spidering the caul, the flies a mob,
we two tramping down the hill, and a desultory cow
alone in the dark.

Red Rosette

Third at the Royal Cornwall, second at Devon County Show,
she was our first cow, and every inch the star.
She arrived to the wild applause of heavy rain,
mud sluicing the lane like a red carpet.

In the field she was best against spring grass,
showing off her coat of burnt sienna or deep rose,
her eyes saying "What goes on behind the scenes
to create a look like this, darling, none of you know."

She was complicated. Pregnancies came and went.
Then last year a caesar, which almost lost us the vet.
We turn it this way and that but come back to the fact
that whatever she is, Aileen isn't a pet.

Now she sashays out of the stock box and into the race,
up through the metal gates and into the ring
where she circles, once, then looks for the brightest spot
(neck long, chest out, butt tight, stomach in).

Bidders crowd the bars like paparazzi.
Aileen swaggers and poses. What she doesn't see
is her weight in kilos on the digital display.
As she raises her chin and pivots – one, two, three –

I know she is telling herself, "Come on girl, you got
third at the Royal Cornwall, second at Devon County Show,
surely this is a first. Now, turn with the hip, slow,
and point me towards the judge with the red rosette."

Handshake

No wonder our sheep held still, seeing how his hands shook
as he hooked a moccasin over each foot with the one,
gripped at the greasy body of the clippers with the other.

And when he raised an arm to show he was ready for another
or reached behind him to yank on the string of the clicker
or handed me a fleece still warm from its owner

to skirt and roll and tie, and tuck into our woolsack.
After we'd helped him pack the portable rig back on the trailer,
and patched up the handful of nicks on our shorn flock

he took a mug of tea in the yard and spoke of the old times,
two-month tours shearing a hundred a day or more
eating lutefisk and dumplings in the crinkled fjords,

the dogs backing the sheep, each shed as big as a Devon field.
And evenings roistering in the bars, not to mention the maids.
How the smell of sheep dip sank deep to the bone.

Then he folded our cheque inside one corrugated palm,
and corralled my small hand in the other. None of us knew
how much of his handshake was thanks, how much tremor.

The Deal

I was ready to trade
the farm, the barns, some mediocre land,
with this moneybags London dude.

So we stood in the yard old-style
about to shake hands on the deal
our fingers just microns apart when the first
tile
fell.

I saw doubt on his face, in his mind,
but too late to check the momentum of his hand
and I grabbed it and held on hard

as the crack in the barn wall yawned
and the slate rubble started to slide
and he saw in my eyes

spring grass too late for a hungry beast,
summer sheep festooned with flies,
autumn keen to surrender the year's lease

and winter's lonely expanse,
the only noise
the strangled klaxon call of the wild goose.

I shook his hand – once – and said, "Fact,
in these parts this is a contract,
big shot,"

and with the help of my Holland & Holland side-by-side
I welcomed him to my world.
After all, what's a man worth if not his word?

Viaticum

When one arrives at the pearl-grey galvanised gates
it falls to Pete to administer the last rites:
decipher the logbook, drain the tank and radiator,
disconnect the battery, the starter motor, the alternator,
take off the fuel pump, trace the registration plate
and enter it under 'currently breaking' on the website.

Each carcass offers up its various hurts: a cracked block,
broken axle or drive shaft, a rusted-out gear box,
evidence of rollovers, jack-knifings, cab fires,
a choked slurry guzzler, a one-armed sprayer.
Diggers are propped on the knuckles of their scoops, or flat out,
their toothless buckets savouring a last mouthful of dirt.

In clean overalls, Pete checks his inventory,
lays them out and anoints each one with WD40.
Once a year Sean the Scrap swings by with his truck
to swap gossip with the blokes in the office out back
and drag out what remains after the necessary cannibalism
and take the relics to Tiverton for the final weighing in.

Cleave Farm

To go back. To climb the hill opposite the house,
that familiar wind cuffing the dry stone wall,
the grass so much come on, the dog cross-
hatching the field chasing timelines of smell,

to look down through layer upon layer of air
at the puckered slate of the stepped mounting block,
the worn lip of the trough, the scours and scars
etched by constant rain on rock,

is to feel both large and small in this panorama
unfolding around us as far as the feet know,
crop and pasture and crop stretching only so far
then telescoping inwards to this moment, now,

for once not ruptured by an animal's terse bray,
dead ducks in the snow, an escaped pig barreling away.

UK364195

Walking winter wheat, the crop kept clean
and fed and watered under a tight regime,
I think of the hundred acres or so of grass
we liked to think of, all these years, as ours.
The cider orchard, bluebells in the copse,
our meadow with its rings of shaggy ink caps,
headlands thick with scutch grass, thistles, ragwort,
a tumble of bones where a struck ewe once sat.
And ask what we've achieved, who were so keen,
or more properly perhaps, what we have done?
Tinkered here and there; let well alone
(though more by luck than judgement or design);
learned more of what we can't do than what we can;
passed on just a little of what we've learned.

*UK364195 – *our DEFRA herd/flock mark*

Fat Hen, Few Eggs

Half the pedigree comes by mouth.
Never knock a farmer with your plate full.
Keep badgers and bankers at arms length.
Speak little, speak well.

A goat in silk stockings is still a goat.
One lawyer makes work for another.
Nearest the heart comes first out.
Garlic is worth ten mothers.

Yesterday's seeds are tomorrow's flowers.
Even a hare will insult a dead dog.
Good fences make good neighbours.
Fat hen, few eggs.

Milk Fever

There's a downner cow in the yard next door,
legs akimbo, black and white body slack.
She's sinking by degrees into the dirt floor,
her calf hungry, her calcium reserves sapped.

I know the symptoms – the pupils blown black,
the stagger as her heart slows, limbs grow cold,
her head bent back and tucked along her flank
as though she's peering over her shoulder.

Not so long ago it would be me out there
saving her life with a syringe and some Calciject,
holding the half-litre bottle high in the air
until my fingers froze and my arm ached.

Now the farmer slips a hypodermic in her
while I, in my own way, with roughshod rhyme,
drip-feed a sort of life back into the old girl
down a two ml line, one word at a time.

Acknowledgements

Acknowledgements are due to the editors of the following journals where some of these poems first appeared: *New Walk Magazine, New Welsh Review, PN Review, Poetry Review, Warwick Review.* Some of the poems were published in the pamphlet *Wheelbarrow Farm* (Templar, 2010). 'Bob's Dogs' is included in *The Best British Poetry 2012* edited by Roddy Lumsden (Salt, 2012).

Thanks to my family and friends, especially my lovely husband, Andy Brodie, our little boy, Inigo, and my three big boys, Jethro, Bruno and Linus. Thanks also to fellow travelers Christopher Southgate and Julie-Ann Rowell, to my tutors at MMU and my colleagues on the MA (especially Khadj) and to Helena Nelson for wise words.

Notes

Pesticides: The World Health Organisation estimates that each year three million workers in agriculture in the developing world experience severe poisoning from pesticides, about 18,000 of whom die. According to one study, as many as 25 million workers in developing countries may suffer mild pesticide poisoning yearly. Children are particularly vulnerable.

Super-weeds: US farmers face a growing challenge from weeds which have developed resistance to chemical sprays such as Roundup due to farmers' reliance on GM corn, soya and cotton. Dow Agrosciences has developed a new type of GM that has resistance to both Roundup and another, older chemical called 2,4-D. 2,4-D is a component of Agent Orange, the defoliant sprayed extensively during the Vietnam War.

Agricultural run-off: Excessive nutrient run-off from agricultural land into rivers and seas causes algal blooms and depleted oxygen, which kills fish and other aquatic life. The Mississippi River, which is the drainage area for 41% of the continental United States, delivers nitrogen and phosphorus into the Gulf of Mexico, creating a dead zone off the coast of Louisiana and Texas. In 2011 this dead zone covered about 6,765 square miles.

Growth hormones: Growth hormones have been used in meat production in the US since 1954; two thirds of beef animals in US feedlots are routinely given steroids and hormones. Studies suggest this can cause early onset of puberty in girls, lowered fertility in men, and increased risk of breast or prostate cancer in later life.